Brief Notes

SECURITY

The publications in *Brief Notes* are outlines of core topics of interest to professionals involved in shopping center management. The outlines are capsule overviews of each topic. Many key points are covered, and shopping center examples are provided for further illustration. Core concepts in each area guide you on topics you may want to explore further. Each outline also contains a helpful glossary.

Brief Notes is designed to provide a helpful and informative overview of the topics covered. It is not intended to be a substitute for more extensive learning that can be achieved through attending ICSC educational programs and reading additional ICSC professional publications.

The outlines contained in *Brief Notes: Shopping Center Management:*

- Management Overview
- Finance
- Insurance and Risk Management
- The Lease and Its Language
- Leasing Strategies
- Maintenance
- Marketing
- Retailing
- Security

Brief Notes

SECURITY

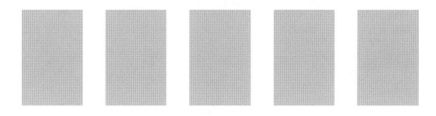

International Council of Shopping Centers
New York

ABOUT THE INTERNATIONAL COUNCIL OF SHOPPING CENTERS

The International Council of Shopping Centers (ICSC) is the trade association of the shopping center industry. Serving the shopping center industry since 1957, ICSC is a not-for-profit organization with over 44,000 members in 77 countries worldwide.

ICSC members include shopping center

- owners
- developers
- managers
- marketing specialists
- leasing agents
- retailers
- researchers
- attorneys
- architects
- contractors
- consultants
- investors
- lenders and brokers
- academics
- public officials

ICSC sponsors more than 200 meetings a year and provides a wide array of services and products for shopping center professionals, including deal making events, conferences, educational programs, accreditation, awards, publications and research data.

For more information about ICSC, write or call the
International Council of Shopping Centers
1221 Avenue of the Americas
New York, NY 10020-1099
Telephone: 646-728-3800
Fax: 212-589-5555
info@icsc.org
http://www.icsc.org

Companies, professional groups, clubs and other organizations may qualify for special terms when ordering quantities of more than 20 of this title.

Published by
International Council of Shopping Centers
Publications Department
1221 Avenue of the Americas
New York, NY 10020-1099

ICSC Catalog No.: 242

ISBN: 1-58268-028-0

Contents

Preface vii
Acknowledgments ix

Securing the Center 1
The Security Process 3
Standard Operating Procedures Manual 5
Keys to Improved Security Policy 9
In-House vs. Contract 11
    The Security Officer 11
    Contracted Security 12
    Proprietary Security 12
    Recruitment 12
    Selection 13
    Training 13
    Promotion 15
    Retention 15
    Off-Duty Police 16
Legal Issues 18
    Civil Liability 18
    Criminal Liability 19
    Foreseeability 20
    Center Security and Liability 20
Community Relations 22
    Police Departments 23
    Fire Departments 23

Record Keeping 24
  Investigation 25
Pin Maps 25
Weapons 26
  Lethal-Weapons Policy 27
  Nonlethal Weapons 27
Bomb/Terrorist Threats 28
Banning and Criminal Trespassing 30
Conclusion 31

Glossary 33

Preface

Security is often defined as the protection of an organization's assets. In a shopping center, the assets to be protected include (1) people, (2) property, (3) money and negotiable documents, (4) information and (5) continued patronage of the customer. These assets are protected by (1) discouraging crime from happening and (2) preserving property and retail activity.

Although each tenant is responsible for the security of his store space, the establishment of indoor and outdoor common area protection at large shopping centers is usually the burden of the center manager. A security program is typically outlined in the *Standard Operating Procedures Manual.*

Becoming more knowledgeable about security need not be a hard task. This book details key points that will help you—the shopping center professional—better understand security management. Important phrases and concepts are clearly defined. A glossary section is also included.

We note that the security issues discussed in this book apply to enclosed malls and possibly to large open-air centers. Strip centers, especially smaller ones, do not have the type of on-site security programs described in this book.

It is not the purpose here to assign legal responsibilities for the elements of security discussed. Rather, this is a detailed overview of the security process, offered to enhance the security environment of shopping centers, for the benefit of landlords, tenants and, most importantly, shoppers.

Acknowledgments

The material in this outline is based in part on a course presented at the International Council of Shopping Centers (ICSC) John T. Riordan School for Professional Development Management Institute.

The International Council of Shopping Centers gratefully acknowledges the individuals mentioned below, who have contributed their expertise to this publication.

James Joly, Vice President, Business Development, Allied Security

Daniel Passarello, SCSM, SCMD, CLS, Director of Mall Operations, Vornado Realty Trust

Donald W. Story, Consultant, Crown American Realty Trust

C. David Zoba, Executive Vice President & General Counsel, Galyan's Trading Company, Inc.

Core Concepts

✓ Landlord vs. tenant responsibility

✓ Coordinating with law enforcement

✓ Areas to monitor

SECURING THE CENTER

Shopping center security is the protection of all assets associated with a center. Security officers do not have police powers, and security policy and procedures are not necessarily designed to enforce civil codes or laws but to protect the shopping center and its assets. Some code enforcement may be expected: for example, no-smoking laws.

Normally, security within a large shopping center is divided between the tenant and the landlord.

The lease document establishes security responsibility between the landlord and the tenant. Usually, the tenant is responsible for the protection of assets within his leased space, while the landlord or center manager must maintain security for the common areas of the center. For example, security from shoplifting within a store space is usually the responsibility of the tenant. Protection from car theft in the parking lot is the duty of the center manager.

However, overall security of a shopping center is largely the burden of a center manager. For example, if a team of shoplifters is moving from store to store within a center and a tenant asks for assistance, center security, in coordination with local enforcement agencies, must comply.

Among the areas of a shopping center that may be the responsibility of the management security team to patrol are:

- Indoor common areas
- Parking lots and decks
- Loading bays, docks and other such areas
- Shared storage areas
- Stairwells
- Roof-access areas
- Fences and alleyways
- All areas of the center after stores are closed.

Core Concepts

✓ Customer and employee safety

✓ Discourage crime

✓ Protect property in common area

THE SECURITY PROCESS

A security program is usually designed to protect the assets of the shopping center in the following ways:

- Safety of customers and tenant employees: For example, customers expect reasonable protection from robberies in the common area of the center.
- Discouragement of crime: For example, the presence of a uniformed security officer in a common area may deter a criminal from acting.
- Preservation of the assets of the center: Shopping center preservation includes (1) protection of property (for example, by establishing bomb-threat procedures and adequately training personnel on how to respond, center manage-

ment better protects the physical plant of the center), (2) protection of retail business activity (for example, a security program designed to limit car thefts in the parking lot will help maintain consumer patronage of the center) and (3) increase awareness of possible terrorist activity, and how to respond to incidents if they occur.

> # Core Concepts
>
> ✓ Security manual contents
> ✓ Duties of security force
> ✓ Community and tenant relations

STANDARD OPERATING PROCEDURES MANUAL

Security policy and procedure are the written guidelines that instruct security officers and management staff on how to protect a center. Policy and procedure can be recorded in a *Standard Operating Procedures Manual (SOP)*. The SOP is often augmented by training materials focusing on security officer training and emergency conduct. Although SOPs will vary greatly from region to region and center to center, most include the following points:

- Employee procedure and conduct: This is the section of the SOP that informs security officers of the duties they will perform and how they will act toward each other, the

---

center staff, consumers and tenants. It may include topics such as:

—Dress codes: Criteria for the type of uniform security officers wear while on the job

—Discipline: Rules and regulations security officers follow while on duty

—Chain of command: An outline informing the security officer staff about whom to report to and take orders from.

- Outline of general duties: This part of the SOP concerns the daily chores a security officer must know and perform. This section usually includes the following procedures:

—Patrolling: Guidelines for walking a specific area of a center or assignments to a fixed post—for example, items security officers should look for when patrolling a parking lot at night

—Traffic control: A basic outline of how to control traffic within a shopping center

—Obtaining assistance: Guidance on when to call for outside help or assistance

—Reports: A policy that informs security officers about what should be reported and how the reporting should be done—for example, reporting broken lights in the parking lot to a superior

—Property familiarity: Security officers should be thoroughly familiar with the whole center. For example, in the event of a bomb threat or possible terrorist activity, security officers may be part of the search team looking for an explosive device. To be effective, the officers have to know the center intimately and be able to spot items that are out of place.

—Other general duties may include door security, clock rounds, alarm response, desk personnel duties and security maintenance.

■ Special procedures: These are policy and operational guidelines for events that are out of the ordinary. These events fall into specific categories:

—Criminal emergencies: Situations that may call for the search, evacuation or containment of all or part of a shopping center. For example, incidents such as hostage taking, barricaded subject, robbery in progress, kidnapping, shooting, riot, bomb or terrorist threats, etc., are considered criminal emergencies.

—Criminal nonemergencies: Conditions in which a crime may have been committed but center evacuation or containment plans are unnecessary—for example, stolen vehicles, illegal picketing, etc. Natural disaster emergencies may require action on the part of a security officer or center management—for example fires, explosions, tornadoes and electrical failures.

■ Community relations: Most SOPs have a section devoted to security officer interaction with the local community as well as interaction with tenants. This section may address:

—Police departments: The SOP will explain how security officers should cooperate with police officers. It may also cover how policy changes with police intervention. For example, a security officer may be instructed not to intervene in actions that take place off center property. However, if a police officer requires assistance, the security officer may have to break that rule.

—Fire departments: As with police intervention, the SOP will outline steps a security officer may take when aiding the fire department.

—The general public: Steps a security officer should take when having direct contact with the public—for example, courtesy procedures a security officer will follow when answering a consumer's question.

—Be seen by tenants and solicit tenant input, particularly as tenants offer an extra set of eyes and can help act as sort of a "neighborhood watch" in the center.

■ Record keeping: The careful notation of every criminal activity or accident involving potential liability that takes place during a security officer's shift. This procedure usually involves (1) investigation (asking questions of people who actually witnessed the crime or accident) and (2) documentation (the careful recording of all evidence gathered during the investigation).

Core Concepts

✓ Write, review and follow policy

✓ Key relations with law envorcement

KEYS TO IMPROVED SECURITY POLICY

To improve security policy:

- Have the policy written down: The SOP, training policy and emergency procedures should all be recorded in some sort of written format. Every security officer, as well as key maintenance and management people, should have a copy of the book.
- Review and revise policy often: A center should periodically go over the SOP and other guidebooks to make sure they are up-to-date and in line with recent civil litigation and changes within the center.
- Establish a working relationship with local police and fire

departments: Informal, polite contacts with both agencies can keep the center abreast of changes in the laws regarding liability and other forms of litigation. Such relationships may also benefit the center through police department records that provide crime trends. Training resources may also be available through such contacts.

Core Concepts

✓ Traits of an officer

✓ Recruitment, selection, background checks

✓ Training and supervision

✓ Promotion and retention

✓ Using police off-duty

IN-HOUSE VS. CONTRACT

A basic decision to be made in deploying shopping center security is whether to use in-house, contract security or a combination of both.

The Security Officer

The most important element in any security operation is the people who become security officers. Ideally, center security personnel should be courteous, intelligent, efficient and interested in security work. They need not only to be aware and offer protection but also to interact well with customers and tenants.

Hiring personnel who have the proper attitude and deportment will result in the development of officers who avoid potentially litigious situations while providing adequate security. The center may choose to staff a security force either through the use of contracted security officers or through the creation of an in-house, or proprietary, security team.

Contracted Security

Contracted security is the use of security officers and procedures provided by an off-site security company. It is called contract security because of the contract between the company and the center. The contract defines the type of protection a center will receive. Under contracted security, the security company handles the staffing, training and supervision of security personnel.

Proprietary Security

Some centers turn to a proprietary security service. Proprietary staffing involves recruitment, selection, training, promotion, retention and supervision by the center management.

Recruitment

Shopping centers with proprietary security hire security officers through ads placed in local papers or inquiries made through local employment agencies. Other areas that yield security recruits are:

- Local police departments: If requested, local police departments must release their eligibility list of people who want to become police officers.

- Local schools and universities: Many junior and community colleges offer criminal justice programs. You might circulate advertisements for part- or full-time security work among enrolled students.
- Retired police officers.

Selection

The paring down of recruits to find security officers must be done carefully. In addition to having the physical and organizational ability to perform security work, the security officer must also possess mental and emotional stability.

Security recruits must be screened before hiring. Among the steps the screening process may have:

- Background and reference check
- Aptitude testing: This may involve a written examination that determines if a recruit has the mental and emotional ability needed to be a security officer. The test is usually administered by a psychologist.
- State registration where required.

Training

Security officers may be taught security programs through careful study of the *Standard Operating Procedures Manual*. A training program may also include:

- Supervision: An instructor usually oversees the training of a new security officer. The instructor can be part of the established security force or an outside expert. For example, many centers train security officers by using qualified security teachers rather than have a senior member of the security staff give informal instruction. Local police assistance may be obtained.

- Structured training: A list of items the security officer should know to be considered fully trained
- Periodic testing
- Discussion: One-on-one meetings between center staff and new security officers to make certain that security procedures have been taught and learned
- Refresher courses
- Training records: The documentation of all instruction given to a security officer. A training record may be used as evidence in favor of a center landlord if a charge of negligent training is brought during a litigation procedure. Documentation may include the title of the training procedure and the date and time it occurred: the name, rank and title of the instructor; what took place at the training and what was taught; and a list of people who attended the training.
- Hours and types of training may be set as part of state requirements for licensing.

Other sources that may be tapped to help keep security officers working at top efficiency may include:

- Contact with local universities: Some local community colleges or criminal justice programs may offer courses that security officers might find worth attending.
- Contact with a local law enforcement agency: Often, if requested, an expert from the prosecutor's office or your local law enforcement agency will come and lecture on legal issues and ways to avoid potential liability.
- Written information: A collection of magazine and newspaper articles concerning security clipped by the center manager and given to the security officers

- Videotapes
- Licensed security training that meets state requirements.

Promotion

Promotion is the advancement of a security officer, based on a system of merit or seniority.

The following factors may also affect the decision to promote a security officer:

- Leadership ability
- Teaching ability
- Continuing education: A security officer of short tenure may be promoted above an officer of longer tenure because of a better education. For example, an officer who attends night school and takes extra courses on security may be promoted before an officer who has been on the job longer.

Retention

Normally, security officers who efficiently perform their duties are kept on as employees. However, any security officer can make mistakes. What determines the officer's continued service is how a center judges the severity of these errors. Among the criteria that may lead to termination of a security officer are:

- Poor work record: This may include, for example, lateness or sleeping on the job.
- Poor disciplinary record
- Use of too much force: For example, although a shoplifting subject runs from a security officer and has to be forc-

ibly arrested, the officer should not use more force than necessary to stop and arrest the subject. Use of too much force may lead to a lawsuit.

Off-Duty Police

Some centers rely on off-duty police officers for the bulk of security staffing. Using police officers has a number of potential advantages and drawbacks. Among the advantages are:

- Firearm training: Knowing how to properly use firearms
- Police officer powers: For certain security assignments, centers may require officers with the power to arrest. For example, when dealing with unruly teens, the center may want an off-duty, uniformed police officer who is familiar with local youth or gang problems.
- Emergency training: Knowing what to do in certain situations. For example, if shots are fired in a center or hostages are taken, a police officer will know what to do until additional police personnel arrive.

However, relying on police officers for center security duty has drawbacks:

- Attitude: Security work is different from police work. Some off-duty officers may not have the understanding or attitude needed to perform all the tasks required of a security officer.
- Divided loyalty: A police officer's first allegiance is to the police department and the community, not to the center. For example, if a tornado strikes, chances are the police officer will be called away from part-time center duty to provide protection for the community, leaving the center with one fewer security officer during a vital period.

- Scarcity: When there are labor shortages, police departments may crack down on the amount of time police officers may take on additional work, diminishing the labor pool for shopping center work.
- Liability: Escalating liability issues may force many departments to limit the types of jobs an off-duty officer can perform. One sometimes-banned area is security work.

LEGAL ISSUES

A major part of any security program is the limiting of potential liability. It is important that a center manager have a basic understanding of liability and how it affects security policy and procedures.

Liability is a state of being legally obligated or responsible. Liability takes on two forms—civil and criminal—both of which have an impact on shopping center security.

Civil Liability

Civil liability is the legal responsibility that one citizen has to another. It applies to an individual who is considered a victim even though no law has been broken. For example, if a person slips on a wet center floor, suffers an injury and brings a lawsuit against the center, the center may be held liable to the person who suffered the injury even though no crime was committed.

Civil liability is determined in a civil suit brought in a civil court of law.

Criminal Liability

Criminal liability is the liability an individual incurs when he or she breaks the law.

Although in some crimes another individual is harmed, the crime is considered a crime against society in general, and it is up to a prosecuting attorney to seek redress in a criminal court of law.

Usually criminal liability results from a voluntary act or an omission to perform a certain duty. It requires that the perpetrator have a mental state of intent, knowledge, recklessness or gross negligence. Mistakes can be a valid defense against criminal liability if they negate one of the requirements.

It is possible to have both civil and criminal liability in the same incident: for example, a person who is mugged and injured on center property. The victim will likely seek redress from the perpetrator in criminal court but may also file suit against the center landlord in civil court, arguing that the landlord should have taken steps to prevent the incident from happening.

Foreseeability

In the shopping center context, "foreseeability" means that in light of the experience in the community, the center should be aware that a certain type of crime is likely to take place on a property and should take precautions to alleviate the potential. For example, say a person is mugged while walking through a parking lot on the way to a car and center security was not patrolling that area of the lot. A judge or jury may, under certain facts and circumstances, find in favor of the victim and against the center in a civil suit if it is determined that the center should have taken measures to protect the victim against being mugged in that parking lot area, despite the fact that there were frequent security patrols.

Foreseeability remains a largely undefined issue. Centers may consider taking the following actions to deal with foreseeability:

- Be aware of crime trends (particularly local trends)
- Sufficiently warn people of danger
- Be aware of terrorist activity (national) that can affect the shopping center.
- Do everything reasonable to prevent a dangerous incident from happening.

Center Security and Liability

If a security program is professional and effective, liability is minimized and there will be fewer lawsuits. However, if security is lax, the question of liability may be brought up in court. For example, a center security officer fails to inform management of a dangerous condition in the shopping center parking lot, and an accident occurs. The center may be held liable because the officer failed to make a report.

There are other ways a security program can make a center liable for civil or criminal acts, among them:

- Negligent hiring: For example, the center can be held liable for damages if the security officer was hired without the center's checking to see if the person had a past criminal record and the officer commits a crime.
- Negligent training: A center may get into trouble if an ill-trained officer causes harm.
- Negligent retention: Continuing to employ an officer when good judgment indicates the officer should be terminated
- Use of too much force: Assault, improper arrest and illegal search by officers can also cause liability for the center.

Core Concepts

✓ Interaction with police
✓ Coordination with fire department

COMMUNITY RELATIONS

A center manager needs to develop good rapport with local fire and law enforcement agencies. A strong, personal relationship with officials in these departments is important for:

- The potential use of resources for the shopping center: Police and fire departments can provide a center with access to vital information and with experts to train a security staff in various procedures.
- Foreseeability: Police and fire departments can provide information and training that will fulfill some of the foreseeability requirements mentioned earlier.

Police Departments

Police departments can be valuable sources of information and training in the following areas:

- Crime reports: Based on police crime reports that show an increase in car thefts near the center, the center may decide to increase parking lot patrols.
- Property familiarity: The police officer whose beat includes the center will be familiar with the center, which will help in times of emergency.
- Potential recruits
- Background checks
- Experts for security training seminars.

Fire Departments

As with the police, fire departments can be a valuable source of safety information for a center's security staff. Areas in which a fire department may be of assistance are:

- Fire inspections: Knowing center security staff can make these inspections more efficient.
- Fire prevention: A security staff properly trained in fire prevention may catch potential problems before they become disasters.
- Safety training.
- First aid training.

Core Concepts

✓ Accuracy and timeliness of security reports

✓ Investigating incidents

RECORD KEEPING

Often, litigation against a center can take more than two or three years to settle. For this reason, it is important for a center security operation to institute a thorough record-keeping program. The security incident report is the most basic responsibility for recording an incident, whether or not a claim is made. It should be done accurately and promptly. Followup reports can be made if more information surfaces at a later date. A record-keeping program has two aspects: investigation and documentation.

Investigation

Investigation is a procedure performed by the security staff after a crime or accident has occurred. It involves the following points:

- Location: The specific area where the event took place
- Description of events: The report will describe the events that happened as the officer or witness saw them. If the officer or anyone else witnessed nothing and arrived at the scene after the event occurred, that should be noted. Officers must also describe actions they took when they reached the scene. Include signed statements from as many witnesses as possible, taken as soon after the event as possible.

PIN MAPS

A pin map of the shopping center site is sometimes employed to track various incidents throughout the center to review patterns and help with patrolling by officers. This is usually a plot plan of the center where pins are placed to document incidents.

Core Concepts

✓ Decision to arm or use off-duty police

✓ Baton, stun gun, mace, pepper spray, martial arts

WEAPONS

Armed officers are a rarity in shopping centers. However, depending upon the type of shopping center, the neighborhood where the shopping center is located and the vulnerability of the center, a center may have to consider arming security officers. For example, a large regional center with many entrances, located near a high-crime inner-city area, may be having problems with armed robbery in the common area. The center manager may decide that the only solution is to arm some of the security officers or hire off-duty police where allowed to augment the unarmed security force.

Lethal-Weapons Policy

A lethal-weapons policy may consider the following:

- Type of firearm the officer is to carry
- Type of ammunition to be used
- Safety precautions: For example, guidelines on how a weapon should be stored and when the weapon may be used
- Extra training: For example, a lecture concerning the liability issues involved with carrying or discharging a gun.

Nonlethal Weapons

Centers wishing to arm officers may resort to nonlethal weapons.

The primary nonlethal weapons available to center security staffs are:

- Baton: A long, thin, heavy piece of wood similar to a nightstick or a billy club.
- Stun gun: A small hand-held device that emits a strong electrical charge that can momentarily stun a person. It is illegal in many states.
- Mace: A spray that can immobilize a person for a few minutes. Also illegal in some states.
- Martial arts: A personal self-defense system such as judo.

It is essential that training is in place on the "defensive" use of these nonlethal weapons.

Core Concepts

✓ Train receptionist on how to handle bomb threat

✓ Conduct search

✓ Decision to evacuate

BOMB/TERRORIST THREATS

A shopping center should have a procedure in place to handle bomb and terrorist threats. Bomb threats are not uncommon in shopping centers and large places open to the public. Most bomb threats are pranks, but all should be taken with extreme precaution. Terrorist threats and activity, while common in many parts of the world, are now more prevalent in North America; thus more precaution is necessary in shopping centers worldwide. Among the points such procedures may include:

- A policy of vigilance and precaution, particularly during periods of high and severe local, state or national alert.
- Trained phone receptionists: The person most likely to receive a bomb-threat call should be trained to respond ac-

cordingly. For example, he or she should take note of the caller's accent or dialect and any background noise and be able to contact the right person to report the bomb threat.

- Search: Well before any threat occurs, a specific search team should be organized and oriented to the responsibilties of safe, effective search techniques.
- Evacuation: Plans should be developed and an evacuation team trained. When a bomb is found, the police and/or fire department will order an evacuation. If a bomb is not found, police usually will defer the decision of whether or not to evacuate to the center manager.
- Forms should be available to anyone answering incoming calls that can be easily filled out at the time the call is received.

Core Concepts

✓ Evictions
✓ Criminal trespass warrant
✓ Involving police in violations
  of criminal trespass

BANNING AND CRIMINAL TRESPASSING

S hopping centers are usually private property and state law dictates how people may be evicted and under which circumstances. People who continually cause trouble in a shopping center environment can be banned from the center. However, the banning must follow strict procedural guidelines in order to be legal. Among the acts an offender must commit before being banned are:

- A criminal trespass on private property: For example, if a teenager who causes a disturbance refuses to leave a center after a security officer asks him to do so, the center manager may be able to ban the teen from the center.
- An offense that is dangerous to the general public—for

example, rowdy conduct. If the behavior does not stop after one warning, expulsion and banning may take place.

Banning policy may include:

- A registered letter sent to the offender and/or parents of the offender explaining the offense and the reason for banning
- A copy of the law that allows the center to ban the offender
- The length of the ban
- A statement noting that the police will be called if the banned individual returns to the center.

Precautions to keep in mind when banning:

- If an unreasonable or unlimited amount of time is put on a ban, it may be overturned in a court of law as being unreasonable.
- Banning cannot be indiscriminate or discriminatory. A criminal offense must occur and the banning must follow a set policy.

CONCLUSION

S hopping center security involves the protection of all assets associated with a center. The lease document establishes the security responsibilities of both the landlord and the tenant. The security program itself is designed to discourage crime and to preserve the assets of the center. The *Standard Operating Procedures Manual* offers a written guideline that instructs security officers and the management staff on the specifics required to protect a center. Because security officers are the most important element in any security operation, they should be well-qualified professionally and able to interact well with customers and tenants. Security personnel can be hired on a contract or a proprietary basis, whichever the center determines best suits its needs. Legal issues are a major part of any security plan, so the center manager must understand liability and how it affects security policy and procedures. It is important, finally, for the center manager to keep thorough records and to establish rapport with local fire and law enforcement agencies.

Glossary

The glossary that follows is a listing of key definitions compiled from this outline, with several terms not defined in the outline added for your information. The terms are defined within the context of this shopping center management topic.

Activity report A written record of openings, closings and alarms for a protected area over a set period of time. The report is usually compiled by the security staff.

Alarm system The network of alarms or monitoring devices designed to detect and alert guards to abnormalities within a center or retail space.

Aptitude testing An examination to determine a recruit's physical and mental capability to perform security work.

Banning Policy by which center security is able to bar a lawbreaker from the shopping center for a finite amount of time.

Baton A long, slender but sturdy stick used by center security as a nonlethal weapon. Also known as a billy club or nightstick.

Burglary Forcible entry into a building to commit theft.

Chain of command   The ordering of a security force by rank or importance.

Civil liability   The legal responsibility one citizen has to another. It is liability law which applies to an individual who is considered a victim even though no law has been broken. Civil liability is decided in a civil court of law.

Contingency plans   Procedures to be implemented by security and center staff during an emergency.

Contract security   An outside security force hired by the center manager on a contract basis.

CPR   Cardiopulmonary resuscitation.

Criminal liability   Liability occurring when a person is harmed by someone who is breaking the law. Redress for criminal liability is argued in a criminal court of law.

Documentation   The written or taped recording of the results of an investigation, survey, patrol or any other activity performed by a security officer in a shopping center.

Dress code   Procedure that defines type of dress a security officer is to wear while on duty.

Eligibility list   List of candidates for police employment compiled by local police departments. Candidates most likely to become police officers are at the top of the list. The lists are available, upon request, to the public.

Excessive force   Use of too much force by a guard during the apprehension or search of a criminal suspect. Determined case by case in a court of law.

Foreseeability   In the shopping center context, it means that the landlord should be aware that a particular type of crime is likely to occur on shopping center property.

Holdup alarm   An alarm that indicates a holdup is in progress. This type of alarm is usually silent.

Investigation   Process by which center security officers determine the cause of a crime or accident. This is usually accomplished by interviewing and documented by eyewitnesses.

Lethal-weapons policy   Guidelines by which security officers are to acquire, use, care for and be trained in lethal weapons.

Local alarm   A detection device that, when activated, sounds a noise alarm.

Mace   A noxious combination of organic chemicals in spray form that is used to disable people. Chemical Mace is a trade name. Illegal in many states. An alternate form is pepper spray.

Motion detector   A device that detects the physical movements of an intruder in a protected area.

Natural disaster   An emergency created by an act of God.

Negligence   The act of being extremely careless. The failure to use such care as a reasonably prudent and careful person would use under similar circumtances. If found negligent in a court of law, a center can be held liable for the actions of a guard or a criminal.

Negligent hiring Careless hiring on the part of a shopping center that directly or indirectly causes a crime or accident. If a center is guilty of negligently hiring an employee, it may be held liable for all negative actions by that employee.

Negligent retention Retaining the services of an employee despite a poor work record. The center may be held liable for an employee's action if it is determined that the employee should have been terminated prior to an incident or accident.

Negligent training The careless training or lack of training of an employee for security work. If it is found in a court of law that a center did not adequately train a security officer who causes an accident or fails to perform adequately, the shopping center may be held liable.

Nonlethal weapons Weapons used by center security that, in normal use, cannot kill a human being.

Perimeter protection Devices designed to protect the exterior openings of a shopping center—for example, door locks and window bars.

Plainclothes officers Police officers or security staff allowed to patrol in normal, everyday clothing.

Proprietary security In-house security developed, managed and maintained by the center manager or landlord.

Protected premises A shopping center that has had an alarm system installed.

Psychological testing   An examination performed by a psychologist to determine the emotional stability of a person.

Reports   Written documentation, based on investigation, describing events that took place during an incident.

Robbery   Forcibly taking property directly from another person.

Search procedure   Step-by-step instruction on how to search an entire shopping center.

Standard Operating Procedures Manual (SOP)   The guidelines by which a proprietary security program is established and maintained.

Stun gun   Small, hand-held device that momentarily incapacitates an intruder through the use of an electrical current or charge. Illegal in many states.

Termination   The firing of an employee.

Terrorist activity   Activity that may be conducted by unlawful individuals for the purpose of terrorizing the general population. These activities can be of a significant magnitude such as the terror attacks using commericial aircrafts in the U.S. on September 11, 2001, or small in scope such as a bomb threat, without actually using an incendiary device.

Training record   Written documents that show how a security officer was trained. Includes documentation of written and videotaped security articles viewed and training seminars attended.